Summer Cocktails

BY **PENELOPE WISNER**

PHOTOGRAPHS BY **DANIEL CLARK**

CHRONICLE BOOKS

SAN FRANCISCO

PHOTOGRAPHER'S ACKNOWLEDGMENTS

I would like to give thanks to my wife, Laura, and my two kids, Ellis and Paris, for their love and constant support. I would also like to give thanks to stylist Sandra Settles for her hard work, openness, and flexibility; to my good friend Bebee for her wonderful collection of antiques and the use of her home; and to Williams-Sonoma, Crate & Barrel, and Sur La Table for the use of their wares.

Text copyright ©1998 by Penelope Wisner
Photographs copyright ©1998 by Daniel Clark
All rights reserved. No part of this book may be reproduced in any form
without written permission from the publisher.

Library of Congress Cataloging-in-Publication Data:
Wisner, Penelope
Summer Cocktails / by Penelope Wisner : photographs by Daniel Clark.
p. cm.
Includes indexes.
ISBN 0-8118-2286-9 (hardcover)
1. Cocktails.   I. Title.
TX951.W56   1998
641.8'74—dc21   98-25788
                                           CIP

Printed in Hong Kong

Designed by Haley Johnson Design Company

Distributed in Canada by Raincoast Books
8680 Cambie Street
Vancouver, British Columbia V6P 6M9

10 9 8 7 6 5 4 3 2

Chronicle Books
85 Second Street
San Francisco, California 94105

www.chroniclebooks.com

DEDICATION

To the many friendships developed and deepened in spirited hours around tables laden with good food and cheer.

ACKNOWLEDGMENTS

When the call for help went out, all responded with alacrity and genuine enthusiasm. I would like especially to thank Rick Holden and Peter-Eric Philipp, my neighbors and guardian angels; Kevin Miserocchi, for his years of steadfast friendship; and Leslie Jonath, a believer, supporter, and cheerleader.

TABLE OF CONTENTS

62 RECIPES

CONTENTS

RECIPES

INDEXES

INTRODUCTION

Summertime. Probably the most indelible lesson
of all our schooling: Summer means vacation.
Day after day of endless hours of sunshine and
no responsibility. Going barefoot. Playing tennis
morning, noon, and night. Outdoor movies. No
clothes (or very few clothes). Never being out of
sight of water and most of the time being immersed
in it. Cotton candy and sticky, sweet smells. Fragrant
peonies, fresh corn, ripe tomatoes, and peaches.
Barbecues, clambakes, and fireworks. Soft nights full
of stars and susurrous waves. Singing in the rain
because, for once, it feels warm on our skin, we have on
clothes that don't matter, and there is no place we have to be.

On the outside we look grown up. We are old enough to drink.
But when May is on the horizon, June is not far behind, and
again we feel the old itches. This evening we will pack the hamper,
the children, and some friends into the car. We'll stop at the
train station and leave a note under our husband's or partner's
windshield wiper: "Come join us at the beach for
supper! We'll have a drink waiting for you!"

Appetite often
fades under
summer's hot
sun and
liberal
doses of
humidity. Thirst
increases. You (maybe I should
speak for myself here) want something to gulp.

Something cold. Something maybe even frozen to cool you down fast. Something so lively it almost sets your teeth on edge with its crisp acidity or touch of bitterness. Something that cuts through the tennis dust, salt, and sand.

On hot summer afternoons in Connecticut, when my father took a lunch break from mowing the lawn, Mom would sometimes carry out a tray with a sandwich and a tall glass already beading with sweat that matched my father's face under his beat-up Panama. The contents were golden and small bubbles streamed from the bottom of the glass. This was not his normal glass of milk!

With his first gulp, Dad sighed happily and beamed at us. Another mystery! Dad didn't beam when mowing. My sisters and I pressed around him: "What is it? Can we taste it?" "It's a Shandy Gaff," came the reply and yes, we could taste it—just a small sip. He was not eager to share. Another shock.

I still remember the taste—cold, bubbling, sweet, bitter. And those are the characteristics I still prefer in hot weather, for me, best delivered now by a really good gin and tonic sipped while strolling in the garden before dinner.

Summer drinks taste best when most spontaneous. Since this is a recipe book, it contains drink recipes. They are not gospel. In these recipes, I pay my debts to tradition—it's pretty hard to argue (though I do my best) with success, and classics are classics for good reasons. But even within a generally accepted formula, there is still room for personal preference. I think almost every drink tastes better with lemon or lime or maybe a strip of orange zest added. If you love, love, love really dark, rich rums (I do), use them in your drinks. No one will complain. If they do, make them another drink exactly like the first and they will soon stop.

Pour one part summer's relaxed spirit into an ice-filled highball. Add equal amounts sunshine, good food, friends, and fun. Stir. Drink with toes curled in warm sand.

TOOLS OF THE TRADE:

EQUIPMENT

IN MY FAMILY, MY FATHER HELD THE POSITION OF DRINK MAKER. HE presided from his bar at one end of the house while Mom's domain, the kitchen, was at the opposite end of the house.

Nowadays, the bar is more often than not in the kitchen, and a good thing, too, since you will then not need to duplicate equipment. Some specialized bar equipment is helpful, but not absolutely essential as substitutes can always be jury-rigged. However, good tools designed for specific tasks always make a job easier. A great place to shop for such things as blenders and bar- and kitchenware is a wholesale restaurant supply store. These are often open to the public one or more days a week. The following list describes the equipment I find most useful.

BAR STRAINER: This coil-rimmed strainer is essential for straining ice out of drinks made in a mixing glass or shaker (though most shakers have a large strainer built in, mine—a nifty, '70s-looking number—does not). A kitchen strainer is not convenient. I tried.

BLENDER: A good, powerful blender is a must for making drinks, especially frozen beverages. A stainless steel canister is preferred as it chills quickly. The number of speeds is not important, but muscle is. Not only do powerful machines get the job done faster, they appear to be geared lower, so their whine and whir is lower-pitched thus saving your ears and sanity. Crushing ice is a handy feature to look for if shopping for a new blender.

How fast and how much ice is necessary to turn a liquid into slush depends on many things, the most controllable being the temperature of the ingredients. If you plan a margarita evening, put the tequila in the freezer. If you follow the recipe and you want the drink more solid, add a little more ice and pulse in quickly. Be careful, though: The more ice you add, the more diluted the drink.

BOTTLE OPENER: In an era of twist tops, this bar staple is still necessary for puncturing cans of pineapple juice and sweetened condensed milk.

CITRUS SQUEEZER: Good idea though not essential.

COCKTAIL SHAKER: Yes. Get one. They are easy to use, great fun, and practical as they mix and chill a drink quickly. Unless you often mix drinks for a crowd, a moderately sized shaker is all you need. Look for one that feels comfortable in your hand.

To shake a drink, put a large handful of ice in the base of the cocktail shaker. Immediately pour spirits and other ingredients over the ice. This begins to chill the ingredients. Fit top and lid on base and grasp with both hands. Imagine you are a maestro bartender and shake away. Always keep hold of the lid. To not do so might cause you some embarrassment.

CORKSCREW: For cocktails, a corkscrew is rarely necessary unless you make wine-based drinks. However, I hope you are also a wine lover, in which case a good corkscrew is essential. I like an Ah-So but these take some getting used to. A never-fail choice is the Screwpull.

GARNISHES: As Beth Harris, bartender at The Tasting Room in Sarasota, Florida, pointed out: "Drinks should look great. Often people are having just one and the presentation is an essential part of the theater and fun of drinking." Keep a collection of short skewers on hand for fruit decoration. Make full use of fresh herbs and edible flowers. Keep your eyes open as you shop. You may turn up a packet of paper parasols—funky, but fun. Or wander with an open mind through the children's toy department. For instance, for a particularly potent drink, you might drop a small rubber snake into the glass. Wrap glass stems with flowers or foliage and secure with florist's wire.

Collect novelty ice cube molds. You don't have to be Dom Pérignon to "drink stars" as this inventor of champagne thought he was doing on tasting the first bubbly wine. Just fill a glass with ice made in tiny star molds. You can make fruit purees and freeze them in the molds, or freeze fresh raspberries or strawberries in regular ice cube trays: Put a berry in each space and fill with water. Or buy whole frozen fruit and use it in lieu of ice. You can add a lot to the look of drinks by rimming the glass as you do with salt for margaritas. (See page 15 for how to rim a glass.) Be creative. Aside from salt and sugar, try colored sugar crystals, shaved coconut, finely grated citrus zest, chopped chocolate, raw sugar, or vanilla sugar.

ICE MALLET: If you don't have access to cracked ice, this is nice to have, but slow-going if you need to crush or crack more than a cube or two.

ICE BUCKET: No ice dispenser? Well, then, a thermal bucket is a great invention. For parties, something even larger, such as a cooler, is very handy as you can keep a measuring cup in it to use as a scoop.

JIGGER MEASURE/SHOT GLASS: Very, very, very handy. Have several. I found a terrific little glass one shaped like a measuring cup. It has gradations on it for teaspoons as well as milliliters and ounces. Another good one is double ended with the classic 11/2-ounce jigger size on one end and the 1-ounce pony size on the other.

MEASURING CUPS AND SPOONS: The cup measures won't get much use, but you'll reach for the spoons often. And if you remember that 3 table-spoons equals 1 jigger you can measure successfully with spoons and/or your jigger.

MIXING GLASS: If you have a cocktail shaker, a mixing glass or pitcher is not absolutely necessary, but if you prefer your martinis stirred, not shaken, it is nearly indispensable. The pint beer glass you may already have is a mixing glass by another name.

MUDDLER: Some would consider this essential. To muddle is to stir until ingredients (usually sugar and lime, lemon, or herbs) get all mixed up. (Mixology is like life!) I prefer sugar syrup to sugar, and so dispense with all this muddling.

STIRRERS: I use chopsticks. In any Japantown, they come in every possible color, length, and material.

ZESTER-STRIPPER: This is an extraordinarily handy combination tool. However, it is not essential if you have a vegetable peeler. If you decide to buy a new zester-stripper, take a lemon with you to the store and try out the tool. You will be amazed at the differences between brands.

SOME LIQUID MEASUREMENTS:

$1/4$ ounce = $1/2$ tablespoon

$1/2$ ounce = 1 tablespoon

1 pony = 1 ounce

1 jigger = $1 1/2$ ounces

2 ounces = $1/4$ cup

4 ounces = $1 1/2$ cups

8 ounces = 1 cup

1 fifth bottle = 750 ml = 25.4 ounces (about sixteen $1 1/2$-ounce servings)
1 liter bottle = 1000 ml = 33.8 ounces (about twenty-two $1 1/2$-ounce servings)

THE MORE THE MERRIER:

GLASSWARE

BEAUTIFUL, AMUSING, RUSTIC, DELICATE, CRYSTAL CLEAR, TINTED, RIM-
med with gold, encircled with color, smooth, cut, or etched. Glasses come in an endless
array of designs and each adds to the celebration of drinking.

For most cocktails, three glass types will cover the bases: an old-fashioned (a short,
fat tumbler), a highball (an iced-tea glass), and a cocktail (a stemmed glass with a
flaring, bell shape). The cocktail is specific to its purpose, but a small tulip-shaped
wineglass could substitute. Whatever the shape or name, glasses should be clean and
sparkling to enhance the colors of the drinks.

In hot weather, large glasses are best to accommodate more ice. Choose capacious
old-fashioned glasses of ten ounces or more and highballs with a capacity of at least
twelve ounces. Cocktail glasses should probably hold no more than five ounces since
these drinks are most often just an ounce or two of chilled spirits served without ice.
The glass must have a stem so that holding the glass does not warm the drink.

With their delicate, slim stems and widely flaring bowls, martini glasses exaggerate
the cocktail shape to create an elegant profile and a dramatic presentation. Any cocktail
benefits from such drama, so don't confine these glasses to martinis.

Margarita glasses, to me, have a friendly appearance. They look, appropriately, like
inverted sombreros. Maybe I like them so well because they also look like butter-
scotch sundae glasses. Use them, as well as old-fashioneds and highballs, for any
blended or frozen drink as well as for dessert.

A NOTE OF WARNING:
While I like large glasses, some are gargantuan. It might
take as much as double a single drink recipe to fill one.

TO CHILL GLASSES: Prechilling glasses helps cold drinks stay cold. Most experts say to stash the glasses someplace cold for an hour. But it is rare that during a party there would be room to spare in the refrigerator or freezer for glasses. If you have the extra space, well and good; otherwise, line glasses up on a counter and fill them with cracked or crushed ice. Dump ice out into the sink before pouring in the drinks. If, like me, you lack counter space as well, designate a cooler full of ice as the glass chiller, or convert a cardboard box (such as a twelve-bottle case from the liquor store) into a cooler by lining with a trash bag and filling with ice.

TO FROST GLASSES: There are glasses etched to look as if they were frosted. I vote for these; they never lose their frost! To frost clear glasses, chill them for an hour or so in the freezer. When the glasses are removed and hit warmer air, the cold steams off them forming a frosty coat that lasts some while, depending on how soon they are filled, the temperature of the day, etc. Refrigerated glasses also fog when exposed to warmer air but they warm up quickly. To extend the frost, fill glasses with ice before refrigerating or freezing or fill immediately upon removal.

TO RIM (OR FROST) GLASS RIMS: To be absolutely correct, prechill the glasses, but you can rim without chilling. Pour sugar or salt in a saucer wide enough to accommodate the rim of the glass. Wipe rim of the glass with a lemon or lime wedge. Dip rim in saucer. For a thicker rim, tilt the glass and roll in saucer. Tap glass gently to shake off excess. Rimming may also be done ahead of time, but then care must be taken not to disturb the glasses and knock off any of the decoration.

Other tasty flavors for frosting rims include flavored sugar such as vanilla sugar and turbinado (or raw) sugar; colored sugar crystals; finely chopped chocolate (white or dark), alone or mixed with sugar; shaved and minced coconut (alone or mixed with chocolate and sugar); finely grated citrus zest (best mixed with sugar); or praline powder.

GOOD, BETTER, BEST:
INGREDIENTS

DRINKS ARE FOR THE MOST PART SIMPLE CONCOCTIONS—SCOTCH AND water, gin and tonic. Such simple mixtures require superior ingredients. Everything matters: the taste of the spirit, the taste of the ice, the temperature of the drink, and the looks of the drink.

Buy the best quality spirits you can afford. If you don't know what brand you prefer, invest first in small, 50-ml bottles. A spirits-tasting party is a terrific way to pick your favorites. Once I organized a vodka tasting at the Russian Tea Room in New York. Twelve vodkas! Or you could go to your favorite bar and have the bartender line up small tastes of the various vodkas, gins, etc., on hand. Some establishments specialize in offering many varieties of a particular spirit. For instance, in San Francisco at the Haight Street branch of Sweet Heat Mexican restaurant, you can sample and compare many brands of tequila and mescal.

NOW IT'S CONFESSION TIME: This tends to happen if you have a drink or two so be careful of your drinking companions! I was in the wine business for years and still love and drink the stuff daily. Because of my personal involvement in the industry and having helped to develop several responsible drinking programs, I have used 80 proof spirits wherever possible and limited the amount of spirit in each drink to $1^1/2$ ounces, a standard jigger, or 3 table-spoons, if this is easier for you to visualize. This amount might be less than a standard bartender's manual would recommend.

CITRUS FRUITS: Many of the cocktails in this book call for wedges, twists, and slices of citrus fruits. Make sure to scrub the fruits well to remove any wax, or buy unwaxed fruit. If you have access to Meyer lemons (a sweet lemon frequently available in California), they can certainly be used instead of regular lemons. However, since they are sweeter, you will have to adjust each drink's sweetness to your taste.

TO CUT A GOOD-LOOKING WEDGE (NOT A HAIRCUT): Cut fruit lengthwise into quarters or eighths depending on how large you like your wedges. Trim off ends where the peel is very thick. Lay wedges on sides and cut out central white pithy core. Pick out seeds if any. Wedges may be further cut in half crosswise, if desired. May be cut ahead and stored in a sealed container for several hours to a day.

To cut a twist, use your zester-stripper, and cut a long piece of the peel with the stripper. Otherwise, cut peel from fruit with a sharp knife or a peeler, stack several pieces of peel, then cut into long strips about one-eighth inch wide and about two inches long. Some people tie the twists into knots or cut them very long and arrange them into spirals. The twists must be very thin (free or almost free of the white pith) in order to make them flexible enough to knot.

To cut slices, use a very sharp knife and cut them as thinly as possible if you want to float them in a drink or add them as an ingredient to drinks such as sangria or iced tea. Remember to pick out seeds. Cut slices that you want to perch on glass rims about one-eighth inch thick.

CRÈME DE CASSIS: Several good brands of this liqueur made from black currants are available, including Védrenne and Marie Brizard. The less expensive brand went down the drain.

FLAVORED SUGAR SYRUPS: Several commercial products went down the drain though made by reputable producers. You can make your own sugar syrup (page 76-78), let it cool, and stir in real vanilla extract and/or real almond extract to taste. These will far surpass what you will find readily available.

GRENADINE: When the real stuff, this sweetened juice of pomegranates is jewel red, sweet, and tart. It is well worth seeking out. Two brands I found are Védrenne Père et Fils and Angostura. The Angostura grenadine includes other fruit flavors as well as pomegranate. The Védrenne is all natural, very thick, and sinks like a stone to the bottom of the drink where it lies in a layer, not affecting the color of the other ingredients until stirred in. Artificial grenadine does not do this. Nor does it taste very good.

ICE: Not all ice is created equal. Water becomes a major ingredient in drinks. If you can, make your ice with filtered or bottled water. Even purchased ice is uneven in quality. It may all be called "party ice" but sometimes it's freshly made, sometimes the cubes have frozen into a seemingly solid mass. In some places, purchased party ice is cracked ice; in others, large cubes; and in still others, small cubes. Search out a source for ice that has a fast turnover. Best of all is a source with its own icemaker.

JUICE: Where juice is called for, except cranberry and grapefruit juice, use freshly squeezed whenever and wherever possible. Procuring fresh, sweet grapefruits, in my opinion, is not an everyday occurrence. So to get consistency in flavor, I have a brand of juice I particularly like and buy that.

LIMES: As no doubt you have experienced, some limes provide abundant juice while others are dry and unyielding. Also, the fresh juice is very tart! Sometimes a squeeze of the fresh lifts a drink from the ordinary to the extraordinary, as in the piña colada. Other times, its tartness, in my opinion, can make a drink stir the acid in your stomach in an unpleasant fashion. A simple solution is to use bottled sweetened lime juice or frozen limeade. My preference is for limeade with its more explosive flavor. There are certain drinks, however, where nothing but the bottled juice will do.

MIXES: Take nothing for granted. Read the ingredients on various prepared drink mixes and then decide if you really want to drink them. I found "esters of wood resin" particularly unappealing. I promise that making drinks from scratch takes no more effort than lugging those heavy bottles home from the store. And your drinks will taste fresher. Take a look at a bottle of sour mix. This has nothing strange in it: sugar or corn syrup and citric acid. Sweet and sour. You can make your own with a tablespoon of lemon juice and a teaspoon of sugar.

ORANGE LIQUEURS: Cointreau, Gran Torres, Triple Sec, and curaçao are four types. Knowing which you prefer is a good idea because so many drink recipes include orange liqueur. Most drink manuals, bars, and restaurants employ the less expensive ingredient—Triple Sec or curaçao. The upscale orange liqueurs are not only more expensive, they have more flavor and more complex flavors. You need less and still you get a higher quality drink. Blue curaçao, by the way, is orange curaçao with coloring added.

PASSION FRUIT PULP: This is occasionally available frozen or canned. If you find any—whether fresh, frozen, or canned—grab it. It's a wonderful ingredient for summer cocktails. The fruit concentrates and syrups I tried failed to come close to the intense flavor of the real fruit.

A FEW PARTY PLANNING

TIPS

THE EASIEST WAY TO STREAMLINE A PARTY IS TO DECIDE WHAT YOU ARE doing ahead of time. Just as for a dinner party when you plan a menu and serve everyone the same thing, you do not need a full bar for every event. Leaf through this book for ideas of what might be appropriate and fun and then choose one drink or more. For instance, make margaritas, martinis, daiquiris, Mai Tais, or piña coladas. Have lots of what you serve so your guests have a sense of generosity. If you are making cocktails before a meal with which you will serve wine, plan on just one predinner cocktail for each person.

If you plan on serving cocktails that need to be very cold, such as martinis, you might want to put the gin or vodka in the freezer ahead of time.

Also make sure to have interesting nonalcoholic beverages on hand—either drinks from this book (see The Zone, page 68) or purchased sodas, mixers, fruit juices, herbal teas. Have them easily accessible so no one has to ask specifically for something without alcohol.

Have plenty of bottled water on hand, both still and sparkling. Many people are "two-fisted drinkers," keeping water in one hand and a drink in the other. Especially in summer, people will often choose water before anything else.

For large parties, buy or rent glassware so you don't have to worry about doing the washing up in order to rediscover the kitchen counters.

For wine, remember these rules of thumb: One 750-ml bottle of wine contains about five average servings. One case (twelve bottles) will provide sixty servings.

Always buy more wine and spirits than you think you will need. If you are serving white or sparkling wines, do not chill all the bottles (wine bottles take only about twenty minutes to cool down so you can always chill more as you foresee the need). Check with the store where you purchase your supplies. They will often take returns if in good shape.

A trick for chilling bottled beverages: Turn any sturdy cardboard wine box into an ice cooler (or glass chiller) by folding in the flaps and lining with a large kitchen garbage bag. Place the bottles in the box and fill with ice. To protect labels, you might want to put each bottle in a quart-size plastic bag. A 750-ml bottle will chill in about twenty minutes.

WHAT TO HAVE ON HAND

KNOWING WHAT YOU WANT TO SERVE KEEPS YOUR SHOPPING LIST SHORT and the amount of storage space needed to a minimum. For instance, if you want to serve Kirs—wine and crème de cassis—you must have cassis on hand. Otherwise, don't stock it. Likewise for real grenadine. If you want to serve Tequila Sunrises around the pool this Sunday, you will need grenadine. For piña coladas, you must have coconut cream. Unless you cook Indonesian food, you may not otherwise need it.

What size bottles to keep on hand? Buy the largest size of the spirits you prefer. The high alcohol content of bottled spirits gives them an infinite shelf life. If opened, the flavor does not deteriorate (wine, port, and sherry do deteriorate once opened). If unopened, the spirit does not "improve with age."

Hot on the heels of the success of flavored vodkas come the inevitable copycats: flavored rums, gins, tequilas. Call me a stick-in-the-mud, but I like the original, unflavored spirit that I mix with real yellow-skinned lemons and green-skinned limes. I've never noticed either fruit go out of season. I know that natural, real fruit is in my drink and how much. Plus my drink looks better with that little bit of color.

BUY LARGE BOTTLES:
The high alcohol content of bottled spirits gives them an infinite shelf life.

FOR SUMMER COCKTAIL MAKING, KEEP THESE ON HAND AT ALL TIMES:

NOTE: Lists cannot take into account preferences. If Pimm's is your favorite hot-weather drink, enter it on your "always" list.

Beer
Club soda or seltzer
Frozen limeade as well as frozen or shelf-stable fruit juices
   such as orange, grapefruit, cranberry, tomato, and pineapple
Ginger ale
Lemons, limes, oranges
Light rum, gold tequila, vodka, and gin
Orange liqueur such as Cointreau
Tonic water

FOR MORE OCCASIONAL USE:

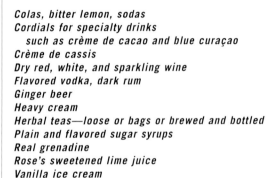

Colas, bitter lemon, sodas
Cordials for specialty drinks
   such as crème de cacao and blue curaçao
Crème de cassis
Dry red, white, and sparkling wine
Flavored vodka, dark rum
Ginger beer
Heavy cream
Herbal teas—loose or bags or brewed and bottled
Plain and flavored sugar syrups
Real grenadine
Rose's sweetened lime juice
Vanilla ice cream
Vermouth, Campari, Pimm's

CHECK YOUR CUPBOARDS. THEY MAY ALREADY CONTAIN:

Angostura bitters
Hot sauce such as Tabasco
Prepared horseradish
Worcestershire sauce

1

SPORTING
TYPES

10 RECIPES

GIN AND TONIC

TO ME, NOTHING SAYS SUMMER BETTER THAN A GREAT GIN AND TONIC. I love the quinine flavor of tonic mixed with the botanical flavors of gin. The drink originated in the tropics where quinine was medicinal and tonic made it potable. Then the English added gin, and a great hot-climate tradition was born. Some people add lemon or lime juice to the drink or garnish the glass with a wedge or slice of citrus; I prefer to squeeze a wedge of lime over my drink and drop it in the glass. Gin is naturally a higher proof spirit (86 proof is the lowest) so be aware of its punch.

1 1/2 oz gin

3 oz tonic water

Lime wedge

Fill highball glass with ice. Add gin and tonic, and stir. Squeeze lime over drink and drop into glass.

MAKES 1 DRINK

BARBADOS SEA BREEZE

A SEA BREEZE IS BEST KNOWN AS A VODKA DRINK BUT IT'S WONDERFUL with rum. The caramel tones of Barbados's rum, Mount Gay, play against the tartness of the fruit juices (as if you needed a reason to drink such good rum!). I tried this with both white and ruby bottled grapefruit juice. The latter, to my taste, makes the drink overly sweet.

1 oz grapefruit juice

4 oz cranberry juice

1 1/2 oz Mount Gay rum

Orange or lime wedge,

for garnish

Pour juices and rum over ice in a highball glass. Garnish with wedge of orange or lime.

MAKES 1 DRINK

LEMONY MINT JULEP

FOR A DRINK AS STEEPED IN TRADITION AS THE MINT JULEP, YOU WOULD
think there must be a one-and-only, absolutely correct way to make it. Here's my version,
but I won't claim it as the best or most authentic. But it is really good.

Plenty of crushed ice

6 oz bourbon

2 oz mint sugar syrup

*(see Herb-Scented Sugar Syrup,
page 78)*

1 lemon, cut into

4 wedges

4 sprigs fresh mint

Straws

If you have silver julep cups, fill
them with crushed ice and place in
the freezer 30 to 60 minutes to
frost. Otherwise, fill 4 highball
glasses half full with crushed ice.

Add 1 1/2 ounces bourbon and 1/2
ounce mint syrup to each glass.
Squeeze a lemon wedge over each
drink and drop in rind. Stir well.
Place a mint sprig and 1 or 2
straws in each glass, then fill to
the brim with more crushed ice.

MAKES 4 DRINKS

CRUSHED VELVET

THIS IS A LIGHTER VERSION OF THE TIME-HONORED BLACK VELVET, A
combination of champagne or sparkling wine and stout. This blend of hard cider and
ginger ale is very low alcohol and refreshing, qualities that make it a great choice for
after sports. Sparkling hard ciders are traditional beverages in apple-rich areas such
as England, northern France, and New England. Like their cousin sparkling pear
cider, they make delicious, low-alcohol drinks on their own.

1 part sparkling hard

cider or pear cider

1 part ginger ale

Pour equal parts cider and ginger
ale into a tall glass. Add a couple
of ice cubes if you like.

MAKES 1 DRINK

SHANDY GAFF

IN HOT WEATHER, ANTICIPATION OF THE COOLING TASTE OF ICE-COLD beer moves our feet quickly toward home from work or play. If anything could beat the flavor of beer (in all its varieties), it would be a Shandy, handed to us without a word of introduction as we walk through the door. This drink, in a nonalcoholic guise with alcohol-free beer, tastes almost just as good as the real thing. Make sure the ginger ale and beer are very cold.

1 part ginger ale
or ginger beer
1 part beer

Pour equal amounts ginger ale and beer over ice in a tall glass. Then bury your thirst.

NOTE: You might want to do some experimenting. Mix various combinations of light or richer beer and ginger ale and try the drink next to one mixed with ginger beer. My favorite combination, probably because it is so closely associated with happy summer days, is a lighter-tasting beer such as Miller and ginger ale.

MAKES 1 DRINK

DARK AND STORMY

BOB FOX, AN EAST COAST SAILOR, SAYS THIS DRINK HAS GREAT MEDICI-nal value: It's a sailors' remedy for upset stomachs. Don't wait to get seasick to try it. So simple and sooooo goooood!

1 1/2 oz dark rum
Ginger beer
Orange wedge (optional),
for garnish

Pour dark rum over ice in a high-ball glass and fill with ginger beer. Garnish with an orange wedge, if desired.

MAKES 1 DRINK

WHISKEY SOUR

AT ONE TIME, THIS CLASSIC DRINK WAS SO POPULAR IT GAVE RISE TO ITS
very own glass shape. A stemmed, small, narrow-bowled wineglass will do the job, as will a
cocktail glass. Variations on the traditional Sour include brandy, Scotch, bourbon, rum, and gin.
The usual garnish is a maraschino cherry, but you won't see one in my glass. Make these drinks
with your preferred type and brand of whiskey—straight, blended, Canadian.

*1/2 oz freshly squeezed
lemon juice
1 tsp Plain Sugar Syrup
(page 76) or sugar
1 1/2 oz blended whiskey
Orange slice and fresh
or brandy-soaked
cherry (optional),
for garnish*

Pour lemon juice, sugar syrup, and
whiskey over a handful of ice in a
cocktail shaker. Shake until very
cold and strain into a chilled,
stemmed glass. Garnish with an
orange slice and cherry, if using.

MAKES 1 DRINK

CAPE CODDER

THIS OLD DRINK GETS A NEW LEASE ON LIFE WITH THE ADDITION OF CITRUS-
flavored vodka. It fascinates me that the all-American cranberry has become
trendy—appearing in everything from fruit-juice blends to teas, cookies, cereals,
breakfast pastries, and sauces for poultry.

*1 1/2 oz citrus-flavored
vodka
5 oz cranberry juice
Lemon wedge
or lemon twist*

Pour vodka and cranberry juice into
a highball glass half full of ice.
Squeeze lemon wedge or twist
lemon peel over drink and drop
into glass.

MAKES 1 DRINK

TOM COLLINS

AS A REALLY PLEASANT SUMMER SIPPER, THIS DRINK HAS SO MUCH GOING for it—from the aroma of gin to the tang of sweet and sour and the fizz of breaking bubbles. Originally made with Old Tom gin, there is room here for your preferred spirit. With rum, the drink is called a Rum Collins; with bourbon or blended whiskey, it becomes a John Collins.

3/4 oz freshly squeezed lemon juice

1 tsp sugar or Plain Sugar Syrup (page 76)

1 1/2 oz gin

About 2 oz club soda

Lemon slice, for garnish

Measure lemon juice and sugar into a highball glass and stir until sugar dissolves, if necessary. Add ice to fill glass halfway. Add gin and stir. Fill with club soda. Garnish with a lemon slice perched on the rim of the glass.

MAKES 1 DRINK

SALTY DOG

FOR YEARS I HAVE BEEN ONE OF THOSE "NO SALT, THANK YOU" PEOPLE. Imagine my chagrin to discover—rediscover—the difference salt makes. Now I want my margarita with salt, and the salt in a Salty Dog is what makes the drink. Maybe salt just makes the drink taste more of the sea. . . .

1 1/2 oz gin

4 to 5 oz grapefruit juice

Pinch salt

Lemon twist (optional)

Pour gin into a highball glass half full of ice. Fill with grapefruit juice, add a small pinch of salt, and stir. Twist lemon peel over drink, if using, and drop into glass.

MAKES 1 DRINK

2

HIGH LIFES

12 RECIPES

OUT IN THE COLD:
THE NEW-OLD TRADITIONAL MARTINI

MARTINIS, TRADITIONALLY MADE WITH GIN, CAME IN MANY GRADATIONS of "dry" depending on how much dry vermouth was added. Then vodka martinis became the rage and still are in many parts of the country. However, gin is so retro, it's in again. If someone insists on a very cold martini, shake it. The drink will have tiny shards of ice in it, increasing the impression of cold. Otherwise, stir the drink. If you add an onion instead of the olive or lemon twist, you have a Gibson.

Splash dry vermouth
2 oz gin
Large green olive
  or lemon twist

Fill a mixing glass with ice. Add vermouth and gin. Stir. Strain into chilled martini glass. Add olive or twist lemon peel over drink and drop into glass.

MAKES 1 DRINK

ESPRESSO MARTINI

THE VERY WITH-IT RESTAURATEUR MICHAEL KLAUBER AND HIS BARTENDER Beth Harris created this martini to celebrate the 1996 opening of The Tasting Room in Sarasota, Florida.

Lemon wedge
2 tbsp turbinado (raw or
  unwashed) sugar
2 tbsp finely chopped
  bittersweet chocolate
2 oz espresso, cooled
1 1/2 oz vodka
1/2 oz crème de cacao
Long lemon twist

Wipe the rim of a chilled, oversize martini glass with lemon wedge. Pour sugar and chocolate into a saucer and mix well. Dip glass rim in mixture and roll to thoroughly coat rim.

Over a large handful of ice in a cocktail shaker, pour espresso, vodka, and crème de cacao. Shake until frothy. Strain into prepared glass. Garnish rim with twist.

MAKES 1 DRINK

THE PURPLE MARTINI

QUADY WINERY, RUN BY ANDREW QUADY, MAKES ONLY DESSERT WINES and they are wonderful. The winery's newsletter reported this delicious martini variation from Boston's Biba Restaurant. It has an intriguing magenta color and flavor. The original recipe calls for a "splash of Elysium." I've changed that to a specific amount to allow both the wine and the spirit to have their say. Elysium, by the way, is a dessert wine that has an aroma of roses and is made from black muscat grapes. It is sweet, rich, and terrific on its own.

1 1/2 oz Bombay Sapphire gin	Pour gin and Elysium over ice in a mixing glass or shaker. Stir or
1 oz Elysium (see Note)	shake until cold. Strain into a
Lemon twist	chilled martini glass. Twist lemon peel over drink and drop into glass.

NOTE: Elysium is distributed nationally, but if you have trouble finding it or want to subscribe to the winery newsletter (*The Dessert Wine Digest*), write or call the winery: Quady Winery, P.O. Box 728, Madera, CA 93639; (209) 673-8068.

MAKES 1 DRINK

007 MARTINI

MORE FROM THE TASTING ROOM. I AM NOT SURE THIS IS WHAT BOND actually drank, but it is suave.

3/4 oz gin	Over a large handful of ice in a
3/4 oz vodka	cocktail shaker, pour gin and vodka.
Lemon twist	Shake until very cold. Strain into a chilled martini glass. Twist lemon peel over drink and drop into glass.

MAKES 1 DRINK

CRANTINI

CAN'T GET ENOUGH CRANBERRY JUICE? IT DOES ADD A REFRESHING FLAVOR.

1 ½ oz vodka
½ to 1 oz cranberry
    juice
Dried cranberries,
    for garnish

Pour vodka and cranberry juice over a handful of ice in a cocktail shaker. Shake well and strain into a chilled martini glass. Garnish with a few dried cranberries.

MAKES 1 DRINK

CAJUN MARTINI

THE DRINK TO PRECEDE A CRAWDADDY FEED.

1 ½ oz plain or
    pepper-flavored vodka
Dash hot sauce
Pearl onion and green
    olive, for garnish

Pour vodka and hot sauce over a handful of ice in a cocktail shaker and shake until cold. Strain into a chilled martini glass and drop in a pearl onion and an olive.

MAKES 1 DRINK

KAMIKAZE

FROM THE NAME, YOU CAN GUESS HOW THIS DRINK IS SUPPOSED TO BE drunk and what it will do to you. Actually, it's so good, I wouldn't want to rush it. And when you take your time, you get to know and like your enemy very much indeed. A New York City bartender claims to have invented the drink to celebrate the opening of *Jesus Christ Superstar* on Broadway. Sometime later, the same drink turned up with the name "Kamikaze," which means "divine wind" in Japanese.

1 oz freshly squeezed lime juice
1 oz Cointreau
or Triple Sec
1 oz vodka
Lime or orange twist (optional)

Pour lime juice, Cointreau, and vodka over a handful of ice in a cocktail shaker. Shake until very cold. Strain into a cocktail glass. Twist peel, if using, over drink and drop into glass.

MAKES 1 DRINK

CORDLESS SCREWDRIVER

SCREWDRIVERS WERE THE FAVORITE WEEKEND DRINK OF MY COLLEGE years, probably because the orange juice disguised the vodka. The drink, in a tall version served with plenty of ice, has been around since the 1950s. This is a hair-raising variation.

Orange wedge
Sugar
1 1/2 oz citrus-flavored or unflavored vodka
Orange twist

Wipe rim of chilled cocktail glass with orange wedge and dip rim in sugar to coat. Pour vodka over a handful of ice in cocktail shaker and shake until cold. Strain into prepared glass. Twist peel over drink and drop into glass.

MAKES 1 DRINK

SWIMMING POOL

YOU MAY LIVE IN A HIGH-RISE, BUT THIS SUMMER YOU CAN STILL HAVE a pool party. Make this totally weird and very good drink for your friends. To be really inviting, a swimming pool must be crystal clear, and so must this drink. So don't use fresh lime juice or limeade, which will make a cloudy drink. Instead, use Rose's sweetened lime juice, available in many supermarkets and liquor shops. The Swimming Pool (also called a Windex—but what's delicious about that?!) was brought to my attention by my friend Ellie Wood. She suggests a toy fish as a garnish.

¹/₂ oz blue curaçao
1 oz Rose's sweetened
lime juice
1 ¹/₂ oz vodka, heavily
iced and strained
Lime slice (optional),
for garnish

Pour curaçao, lime juice, and vodka over a large handful ice in a cocktail shaker. Shake well and strain into a chilled cocktail glass. Perch a lime slice on glass rim, if desired.

BLUE HAWAII: If you've invested in a bottle of blue curaçao, you have proven you have a sense of humor and you will probably want another drink using it. Try a Blue Hawaii (this tasty drink is more than just an excuse to use up the blue curaçao, but perhaps an excuse will come in handy): Pour 1 ounce light rum, 1 ounce blue curaçao, 1 tablespoon freshly squeezed lemon juice, and 2 tablespoons (1 ounce) pineapple juice over cracked or crushed ice in a highball or old-fashioned glass.

MAKES 1 DRINK

GIMLET

THIS IS A CLASSIC DRINK WITH A HISTORY, SHOWING UP IN PRINT FIRST in 1928. I imagine high-heeled women and men in double-breasted blazers drinking these in elegant, smoky clubs. It tastes like a classic, too—clean, well-balanced, timeless. Though the cocktail is slightly hazy when made with fresh versus bottled sweetened lime juice, I prefer the taste of this version. A gimlet is also made with vodka if that is your potion of choice.

1 1/2 oz gin

1 oz freshly squeezed
   lime juice

1 tsp Plain Sugar Syrup
   (page 76) **or sugar**

Long lime twist

Pour gin, lime juice, and sugar syrup over ice in a cocktail shaker. Shake until very cold. Strain into a chilled cocktail glass. Garnish with lime twist in glass or hung over the rim for a rakish look.

MAKES 1 DRINK

COSMO

SHORT FOR COSMOPOLITAN AND SOMETIMES CALLED A PINK COSMO (it is pink), this is a popular drink served in a martini glass. Don't let the color fool you: It's a full-bore drink. In a bar, it's usually made with Triple Sec. Go upscale at home and make the drink with Cointreau.

1 1/2 oz vodka

1 tsp Cointreau or
   1 1/2 tsp Triple Sec

1 tsp freshly squeezed
   lime juice

1/2 oz cranberry juice

Long lime twist,
   for garnish

Pour vodka, Cointreau, lime juice, and cranberry juice over ice into a cocktail shaker. Shake until frothy and strain into a chilled cocktail or martini glass. Garnish with lime twist hooked over rim.

MAKES 1 DRINK

STRAIGHT UP MARGARITA
Frozen Margarita

FROZEN PIÑA COLADA

ESPRESSO DELUXE

ANYTHING GOES DAIQUIRI
FROZEN FRUIT DAIQUIRI
AVOCADO DAIQUIRI

FROZEN GIN SOUR

3

FROZEN FANTASIES

8 RECIPES

STRAIGHT UP MARGARITA

THIS IS AN ADAPTATION OF THE MARGARITAS MADE AT SWEET HEAT, a trendsetting Mexican restaurant in San Francisco owned by the energetic and always enthusiastic Jeff Saad. Saad is first a chef and it shows in his margarita recipe. First he researched, then he experimented, then he tried the drink on his customers, perfecting, perfecting. He discovered that the acidity of fresh lime juice, traditional in margaritas, often overwhelms his customers. He uses Nielsen Frozen Lime Juice. If you can find it, mix it with sugar syrup (page 76) to taste. Frozen limeade is easier to find and you don't need to add syrup or sugar, but can use it straight from the can. Saad also uses top-quality spirits—Cuervo 1800 tequila and Gran Torres orange liqueur. I, too, prefer the mellower and more complex gold and aged tequilas. You can serve margaritas many ways: with or without salt (the bite of salt against sweet and sour becomes addictive!), straight up, shaken, blended, and frozen.

1/4 fresh lime
Kosher salt
1/2 oz frozen limeade
1 oz water
1/2 oz Gran Torres
or Cointreau
1 1/2 oz Cuervo
1800 tequila
Large handful ice

Wipe the rim of a chilled cocktail glass with the fresh lime. Dip glass rim in a saucer of salt. Tap glass to shake off excess.

To shake the drink, put limeade, water, Gran Torres, tequila, and a large handful of ice in a cocktail shaker. Close and shake until frothy. Strain into prepared glass.

You can also pulse the drink in a blender and strain into the glass.

MULTIPLES: Increase ingredients proportionately, but don't make ahead. Make each round fresh.

FROZEN MARGARITA: Use 3 ounces tequila, 1 ounce Gran Torres, 1 1/2 ounces limeade, and 1 cup crushed ice. Measure ingredients into a blender container. Blend until slushy. Serve with a straw and a slice of lime. Makes 2 drinks.

MAKES 1 DRINK

FROZEN PIÑA COLADA

MY NEIGHBORS WERE VERY HAPPY TO JOIN THE RECIPE TESTING WHEN
the subject became piña coladas, their favorite. It is very simple and there is absolutely
no reason I can think of to bother with prepared mixes.

1 1/2 oz coconut cream
(see Note)

3 tbsp crushed pineapple

1 1/2 oz light rum

1 cup crushed ice

1/2 lime

Straw

Measure coconut cream,
pineapple, rum, and ice into a
blender container. Blend until
slushy. Pour and scrape into
a chilled old-fashioned glass,
large tumbler, or highball glass
and squeeze lime over drink.
Discard rind. Serve with a straw.

NOTE: Coconut cream is available canned in specialty food shops or Mexican or Latin American markets.

MAKES 1 DRINK

ESPRESSO DELUXE

IN SUMMER, COFFEE SHOPS VIE WITH EACH OTHER TO DEVELOP FROZEN
coffee drinks to slake hot-weather thirsts. This is my version inspired by Spinelli's Spin.

2 oz cooled espresso

2 oz sweetened
condensed milk

About 12 espresso
beans (optional)

1 1/2 cups crushed ice

1 1/2 oz orange-flavored
Stolichnaya, or
1 1/2 oz vodka and
3/4 tsp Cointreau

Straw

Measure espresso, condensed milk,
espresso beans (if using), ice, and
vodka into a blender container.
Blend until slushy. Pour and scrape
into a very large glass and serve
with a straw.

MAKES 1 DRINK

ANYTHING GOES DAIQUIRI

AN AMERICAN ENGINEER WORKING THE MINES IN A TOWN CALLED
Daiquiri, Cuba, at the turn of the 20th century may have invented or named the daiquiri.
Havana's La Florida Bar is credited with perfecting the frozen daiquiri and several variations.

¹/₂ oz frozen limeade
1 to 1 ¹/₂ oz water (see Note)
1 ¹/₂ oz light rum

Measure limeade, water, and rum
into a shaker with a large handful of
ice. (For a frothier drink, put ingredients in a blender and pulse quickly
once or twice.) Shake well and strain
into a chilled cocktail glass.

NOTE: The larger amount of water produces a slightly less acidic drink.

MAKES 1 DRINK

FROZEN FRUIT DAIQUIRI

YOU CAN ALSO TRY THIS DRINK WITH MIXED LIGHT AND DARK RUMS.

1 oz frozen limeade
2 oz light rum
Fresh fruit such as
    1 medium banana,
    ¹/₃ cup crushed
    pineapple,
    ¹/₂ cup cubed mango,
    sliced strawberries,
    or raspberries
1 cup crushed ice
Fresh fruit, for garnish
Straws

Measure limeade, light and dark
rums, fruit, and ice into a blender
container. Blend until slushy.
Pour into an old-fashioned glass or
a large tumbler. Garnish with fresh
fruit and serve with straws.

MAKES 2 SMALLER DRINKS OR 1 VERY LARGE DRINK!

AVOCADO DAIQUIRI

RUM, LIME, AND AVOCADO. YUM! THIS MAY BE MY FAVORITE. USE RICH
Haas avocados. This is an adaptation of a drink Joe Carcione created for his
Greengrocer Cookbook. At some point in the experimenting with daiquiri varia-
tions—and I don't know where that point is exactly—daiquiris may stop being
daiquiris and be something else. You could call your drink your Summertime Special.
Whatever the name, it will taste great!

1 oz frozen limeade	Measure limeade, rum, avocado,
1 1/2 oz light rum	and ice into a blender container.
1/4 medium avocado	Blend until slushy. Pour and scrape
1 cup crushed ice	into an old-fashioned glass or large
Lime wedge, for garnish	tumbler. Garnish with lime wedge
Straw	and serve with a straw.

MAKES 1 DRINK

FROZEN GIN SOUR

THIS IS A VERY COOL WAY TO DRINK GIN IN THE HEAT OF THE DAY—
or night. Your choice.

1 1/2 oz gin	Measure gin, cream, limeade,
1 oz heavy cream	Cointreau, and ice in a blender
1/2 oz frozen limeade	container. Blend until slushy.
1 tsp Cointreau	Pour and scrape into a chilled
(optional)	old-fashioned glass or highball
1 cup crushed ice	glass. Garnish with a lime wedge
Lime wedge or slice,	or slice, and serve with a straw.
for garnish	
Straw	

MAKES 1 DRINK

NEGRONI

SCOTCH RICKEY

CAMPARI:
CAMPARI AND SODA
CAMPARI ORANGE

LONG ISLAND ICED TEA

PIMM'S COOLER

4

THE
COUNTRY
CLUB SET

6 RECIPES

NEGRONI

WINEMAKERS KNOW A GOOD THING WHEN THEY TASTE IT—TASTING IS
their business. For a number of Northern California winemakers, the Negroni reigns
as their favorite tipple when they escape the prying eyes of those who insist that winemakers always drink wine. The interplay of flavors makes this a great drink to savor.

1 1/2 oz gin

1 1/2 oz Campari

1 1/2 oz sweet vermouth

Lemon twist

Place several ice cubes in an
old-fashioned glass and add gin,
Campari, and vermouth. Stir.
Twist lemon peel over drink and
drop into glass.

MAKES 1 DRINK

SCOTCH RICKEY

RICKEYS ARE A FAMILY OF DRINKS CREATED BY ADDING FRESH LIME
juice and soda or seltzer to your favorite spirit: Scotch, gin, rum, tequila, vodka (have
I forgotten anyone?). It's a refreshing change for summer. When you run out of soda
(or the bottle's gone flat), make the drink with water and it's a Scotch Sling. If the
drink has too much pucker power to suit you, add a teaspoon of sugar syrup or sugar,
though some would consider this a capital offense.

1 1/2 oz Scotch

1/2 oz freshly squeezed
lime juice

Splash club soda
or seltzer

Lime twist

Pour Scotch and lime juice over
ice in a highball glass. Stir and top
off with soda. Twist lime peel over
drink and drop into glass.

MAKES 1 DRINK

CAMPARI

CAMPARI'S JEWEL-LIKE RED COLOR PLEASES THE EYE AND COMPLEMENTS summer's heat, while the liqueur's bitter edge cuts through the dust in the back of your throat. Its low alcohol content, 24% by volume or 48 proof, makes it pleasantly relaxing but not overwhelming, especially when mixed with soda or orange juice. A nice choice to while away long, hot hours.

CAMPARI AND SODA

OTHER THAN ON THE ROCKS (WHICH IS ALSO VERY GOOD), THIS IS THE simplest way to enjoy Campari. The usual proportions are two-thirds Campari and one-third soda. But to make it really refreshing and light, I use the reverse.

2 oz Campari	Pour Campari over ice in an old-
4 oz club soda	fashioned glass. Fill with soda,
Lemon wedge	then squeeze lemon wedge over
	drink and drop into glass. Stir.

MAKES 1 DRINK

CAMPARI ORANGE

YOU WERE UP AT SUNRISE FOR AN EARLY GAME OF TENNIS. NOW IT'S 11 a.m. and time for a drink. With freshly squeezed orange juice, this is one of my favorite drinks anytime of day.

2 oz Campari	Pour Campari over ice in an
4 oz freshly squeezed	old-fashioned glass. Fill with
orange juice	orange juice, stir, and prop an
Orange slice, for garnish	orange slice on the glass rim.

MAKES 1 DRINK

LONG ISLAND ICED TEA

WELCOME TO LONG ISLAND'S FAMOUS BEACH COMMUNITIES! BRIDGE-
hampton, Southampton, East Hampton, Westhampton, and out at the tip, Montauk.
There's a spirit in this drink for each town. How such an incredible mix of spirits
tastes like sweet, orange-laced tea is a mystery. Using Triple Sec instead of Cointreau
gives a sweeter, less pronounced orange flavor.

½ oz light rum
½ oz vodka
½ oz gin
½ oz gold tequila
½ oz Cointreau or
  Triple Sec
½ oz freshly squeezed
  lemon juice
Splash cola
Orange or lemon wedge,
  for garnish

Over ice in a highball glass, pour
rum, vodka, gin, tequila, Cointreau,
and lemon juice. Stir, and add a
splash of cola for color and to round
the flavors. Garnish with orange or
lemon wedge.

MAKES 1 DRINK

PIMM'S COOLER

PIMM'S IS A TERRIFIC SUMMER APERITIF. IT HAS A DEEP, COMPLEX FLAVOR
that plays with bitter and sweet, herbal and fruity. I have a feeling people forget about
Pimm's and that's too bad. Let this be a reminder to put it on your summer menu.

1 ½ oz Pimm's
1 ½ to 3 oz ginger ale
  or lemon-lime soda
Lime wedge

Pour Pimm's and ginger ale into a
highball glass half-filled with ice. For
a more intense flavor, use the lesser
amount of mixer. Squeeze lime
wedge over drink and drop into glass.

MAKES 1 DRINK

MAI TAI

TROPICS

TEQUILA SUNRISE

RIVIERA

PLANTER'S PUNCH

BY THE
POOL

5 RECIPES

MAI TAI

THE REFERENCE BOOKS SAY TRADER VIC INVENTED THE MAI TAI AT his Hinkey Dinks Restaurant in Oakland, California. However, Hawaii and drinking Mai Tais are inseparable. I use Whaler's, the delicious, dark Hawaiian rum.

1 1/2 oz light or dark rum

1/2 oz Cointreau

1/2 oz Almond Sugar Syrup (page 76)

1/2 oz real grenadine

1/2 oz freshly squeezed lime juice

1 tsp pineapple juice

Fresh pineapple spear, for garnish

Straws

Put a large handful ice in a cocktail shaker. Add rum, Cointreau, almond syrup, grenadine, lime juice, and pineapple juice. Shake well and strain into a chilled old-fashioned glass full of ice. Garnish with a pineapple spear and serve with 1 or 2 straws.

MAKES 1 DRINK

TROPICS

THE BOOK DOESN'T SAY WHETHER ROBINSON CRUSOE BUILT HIMSELF A
still. But if we think about what we might really want on a desert isle, some rum and fresh fruit
sounds like a very good idea. This drink could turn an afternoon at home into a tropical fantasy.

1 1/2 oz pineapple juice	Measure juices, grenadine,
1 1/2 oz freshly squeezed	banana, rum, and ice into a
orange juice	blender container. Blend until
1/2 oz freshly squeezed	pureed. (Texture will be thick
lemon juice	but not frozen.) Pour into
1/2 oz real grenadine	a large old-fashioned glass,
1/2 medium banana	then squeeze lime wedge over
1 1/2 oz dark rum	drink and drop into glass.
1/2 cup crushed ice	Serve with 2 straws.
Fat lime wedge	
Straws	

MAKES 1 DRINK

TEQUILA SUNRISE

SUNRISE TO SUNSET, THIS DRINK IS DESERVEDLY POPULAR. IT TAKES ITS
name from layers of orange juice and red grenadine. Fresh orange juice lifts the drink into the
realm of something special. So does real grenadine!

1 1/2 oz Cuervo tequila	Pour tequila, orange juice,
4 oz freshly squeezed	and lemon juice over ice in a
orange juice	tall highball glass. Stir, then
1/2 oz freshly squeezed	add grenadine slowly so it settles
lemon juice	to the bottom of the glass.
1/2 oz real grenadine	Garnish with an orange slice
Orange slice, for garnish	and serve with a swizzle stick.
Swizzle stick	

MAKES 1 DRINK

RIVIERA

THIS VERY CHIC DRINK HAS AN ACID YELLOW-GREEN COLOR, WITH AN intriguing interplay of anise and grapefruit flavors. Pernod, with its strong, distinctive flavor of anise, may be an acquired taste. But if you love the powerfully evocative sights, sounds, and smells of Marseilles, then you probably also have a taste for its local quaff.

1 1/2 oz Pernod *3 oz grapefruit juice* *Lemon or lime twist*	Half fill a highball glass with ice. Add Pernod and grapefruit juice and stir. Twist lemon or lime peel over drink and drop into glass.

MAKES 1 DRINK

PLANTER'S PUNCH

THERE MUST HAVE BEEN A TIME IN CARIBBEAN HISTORY WHEN EVERY plantation owner's hospitality depended on the reputation of his Planter's Punch.

1 1/2 oz dark rum
1/2 oz real grenadine
1 tsp Cointreau
2 tsp pineapple juice
1/2 oz each freshly
   squeezed lemon and
   lime juice
1/2 oz Plain Sugar Syrup
(page 76)
Club soda
Lime slice (optional),
   for garnish
Straws
	Put a large handful ice in a cocktail shaker. Add rum, grenadine, Cointreau, juices, and sugar syrup. Shake well. Strain into a highball glass half full of ice. Top off with club soda. Garnish with a lime slice, if desired, and serve with 1 or 2 straws.

MAKES 1 DRINK

6

THE
BRUNCH
BUNCH

11 RECIPES

KIR AND KIR ROYALE

IN FRANCE, WHERE IT IS TRADITIONAL TO SCOUT THE LOCAL WOODS FOR whatever is in season, many homes gather wild berries and preserve them in a syrup of wine and sugar. In Burgundy, not only is the wine extraordinary, so are the black currants. The Burgundians make a liqueur from these berries called crème de cassis. Unless you have a homemade syrup, a fine crème de cassis such as that from Védrenne Père et Fils, or a similar American product such as the framboise from California's Bonny Doon Vineyard, I would skip this drink altogether. It's an ideal aperitif for a weekend lunch or brunch, before supper at the beach, or on the deck. And just because you are adding something sweet to sparkling (Kir Royale) or still wine (Kir) does not mean the wine can be ordinary. Choose something well balanced and palatable that you enjoy on its own merits.

1 to 2 tsp crème de cassis

About 5 oz chilled champagne, sparkling wine, or dry white wine

Pour 1 or 2 teaspoons, to taste, cassis in the bottom of a flute or tulip-shaped white-wine glass. Fill with cold champagne.

MAKES 1 DRINK

BELLINI

THE CREATION OF HARRY'S BAR IN VENICE, THE BELLINI IS A STUDY IN the science of simplicity: simple and elegant, simple and rare, simple and surprising, simple and delicious. Luckily, white peaches, the traditional ingredient, are becoming more widely available thanks to enterprising farmers and farmers' markets. A very good Bellini may also be made with fresh yellow peaches. Just be sure the peaches are exquisite—perfectly ripe and highly aromatic. No mealy-mouths allowed. The wine should be delicate, crisp, and lightly fruity.

¹/₄ ripe peach, peeled and cut into thin slices

Sparkling wine

Drop peach slices into a tall, slim flute and fill with sparkling wine.

MAKES 1 DRINK

A MEAL IN ITSELF: BLOODY MARY

THE BLOODY MARY IS EQUALLY BELOVED BY BRIDGE CLUBS, BRUNCH guests, and anyone who likes a snack before lunch. There have to be more variations on this drink than there are for gazpacho. And, come to think of it, if you have a favorite gazpacho recipe, just add vodka, and you will have an original and fabulous drink! Nearly all the accompanying ingredients in a Bloody Mary are optional. This version was given to me by San Francisco bartender Joe D'Alessandro, but no amount of sweet talk would make him part with a last secret ingredient. As it is, it tastes spicy, full-flavored, and will encourage you to keep trying variations until you find your own secret ingredient.

1 1/2 oz vodka

4 to 5 oz tomato juice

Dash hot sauce such as
*   Tabasco, Louisiana Hot*
*   Sauce, or, for variety,*
*   one of the green/jalapeño*
*   hot sauces*

1 1/2 tsp prepared horseradish

1 tsp Worcestershire sauce

Salt and freshly ground
*   pepper, to taste*

Lemon wedge

Pinch celery salt (optional)

Pickled green bean
*   or asparagus spear,*
*   for garnish*

In a generous glass such as a tall highball half full of ice, stir together vodka, tomato juice, hot sauce, horseradish (yes, it's a good dose, but I won't call you names if you leave it out or use less), Worcestershire, salt, and pepper until well blended. Squeeze lemon wedge over drink and drop into glass. Stir again. Dust top with celery salt, if using, and garnish with a pickled green bean or asparagus spear.

BLOODY MARIA: Use tequila and a lime wedge instead of vodka and lemon.

DANISH MARY: Substitute Akvavit, a caraway-flavored spirit, for vodka.

EVEN SPICIER BLOODY MARY: Use a pepper- or chili-flavored vodka.

VIRGIN MARY: Omit the vodka and you have the designated driver's best friend.

MAKES 1 DRINK

PASSIONATE MIMOSA

THIS WOULD BE A DELIGHTFUL DRINK TO FIND ON A BREAKFAST TRAY. IF
you want to gild the lily (so to speak), cut an apricot-colored garden rose (pesticide-free,
of course!) to use as a swizzle and take it to your beloved. Just make sure to trim the
thorns or your sweetie might not be so happy.

1/2 oz orange/passion
fruit frozen juice
concentrate or passion
fruit sorbet
Sparkling wine
Long orange twist
Fresh raspberry

Place juice concentrate in the
bottom of a champagne flute. Fill
glass with sparkling wine and stir
lightly. Drop in twist and raspberry.

MAKES 1 DRINK

BRIDESMAID

JUST LIKE ITS HUMAN COUNTERPART, IT'S IRRESISTIBLE. PINK AND VERY,
very pretty. If you are looking for the ideal drink for a bridal shower, a baby shower,
the bridesmaids' breakfast, this is it! Rim and frost the glasses ahead of time if you
have a spot to store them safely until serving time. In a pinch, omit frosting and just
rim the glasses. Just make sure the ingredients are all good and cold.

Lime wedge
Pink or white sugar
crystals, or a mixture
of both
Small scoop (about
2 tbsp) raspberry sorbet
2 oz ginger ale
4 oz sparkling wine

Wipe rim of a well-chilled margarita
glass with lime wedge, then dip
rim in sugar crystals to coat. Scoop
sorbet into glass. Then carefully
pour in ginger ale down side of
glass so it does not foam too much
as it hits the sorbet. Add sparkling
wine in the same fashion.

MAKES 1 DRINK

SANGRIA

A TERRIFIC LITTLE SPANISH RESTAURANT IN SAN FRANCISCO, ZARZUELA, serves this delicious sangria. Make it a few hours ahead to allow the flavors time to meld. The whole fruits added to the mix are more suggestions than requirements. Why not take happy advantage of summer's bounty, especially ripe peaches and nectarines? If you happen to use frozen, sweetened fruit, go easy, as their extra sugar can easily take the sangria over the top in terms of sweetness. You may strain the macerated fruit out of the sangria and serve it separately, if desired, or if you don't like to watch your guests fishing in their glasses for pieces of fruit with their fingers or forks. Naturally, that's the part of sangria I enjoy most.

2 cups sugar

1 cup water

Peeled zest of 2 oranges

Peeled zest of 2 lemons

1 small cinnamon stick

750-ml bottle

  dry red wine

2 oz brandy (see Note)

1/2 oz Gran Torres or

  Triple Sec (optional)

1/2 orange, thinly sliced

1/2 lemon, thinly sliced

1/2 crisp apple, unpeeled

  and thinly sliced

Handful whole fresh

  strawberries

Bring sugar, water, orange zest, lemon zest, and cinnamon stick to a boil, while stirring, in a heavy saucepan over medium-high heat. Lower heat to medium and simmer, uncovered, 5 minutes. Strain syrup into a container, let cool, cover, and refrigerate until needed. Makes about 1 1/2 cups flavored syrup. Keeps indefinitely but may begin to crystallize over time.

Several hours before serving, in a pitcher mix together wine, brandy, 1/4 cup syrup, and Gran Torres, if using. Add fruits and refrigerate until ready to serve. Pour over ice.

NOTE: The type of brandy you use will have an effect on the flavor of your sangria. For best results, choose a smooth, mellow (but not sweet), oak-aged brandy.

MAKES ABOUT 6 DRINKS

GINGERY ICED TEA

JOE'S REFRESHER

WATERMELON AGUA FRESCA

BETA-CAROTENE HIGH

FROZEN HONEY LEMONADE AND LIMEADE

HOMEMADE ORANGEADE
Homemade Lemonade

FRESH GINGER ALE

MADRAS
Madras with Spirits

THE
ZONE:
ALCOHOL-FREE DRINKS
10 RECIPES

GINGERY ICED TEA

ON MY FIRST TRIP TO MOROCCO, I WAS SHOCKED TO SEE DJELLABA-
cloaked men drinking small glasses of hot, minty tea on café patios in the full glare of
the sun. Long clothes and hot drinks is not how Americans generally cope with heat.
Then I tasted the strong, very sweet, minty tea and understood.

*1 1/2 tbsp loose green
tea or black tea
1/2 cup sugar
1 bunch fresh mint
1 oz fresh ginger,
peeled, thinly sliced,
and lightly crushed
Mint sprigs and crystal-
lized ginger slices
(optional), for garnish*

Bring a teakettle full of water to a
rolling boil. Rinse out a 3-cup or
larger teapot with boiling water.
Fill with tea, sugar, fresh mint, and
fresh ginger. Fill with boiling water
and let steep until cool. Place a
sprig of fresh mint in each tall glass,
fill with ice, then pour in tea. Cut a
slit in slices of crystallized ginger,
if using, and fit onto rim of glasses.

MAKES ABOUT 6 DRINKS

JOE'S REFRESHER

FROM HIS NEW YORK ITALIAN FAMILY, MY FRIEND JOE PICKED UP THE HABIT
of drinking bitter beverages in hot weather, as appetite invigorators and as digestifs after
a meal. Make this in the size glass that fits your thirst.

*Club soda
Ginger ale
1 tsp Angostura bitters
(more or less to taste)
Lemon wedge*

Fill a glass with ice. Fill with soda,
then add a splash of ginger ale.
(Just enough to flavor the soda.
You don't want to turn this into a
sweet drink.) Add bitters, then
squeeze lemon wedge over drink
and drop into glass. Stir and sip.

MAKES 1 DRINK

WATERMELON AGUA FRESCA

IT'S DELICIOUS, FRESH, LIGHT, EASY TO MAKE, AND A GREAT ACCOMPANI-
ment to spicy summer fare. And you don't have to worry about seeds. Make this with
yellow or pink watermelon. You shouldn't need to sweeten the agua fresca if the watermelon has a sweet, ripe flavor. You can make agua frescas with all of summer's melons.

¹/₄ large watermelon	Cut watermelon flesh from rind.
(about 1 ³/₄ lbs)	Put flesh (seeds and all) in blender
1 cup sparkling or	container with the 1 cup water and
still water, plus more	a pinch of salt. Blend until smooth.
if needed	Strain into a pitcher. Taste and
Pinch salt	dilute with more water if you like.
¹/₂ oz lime juice	Add lime juice, if using.
(optional)	

MAKES ABOUT 3 TO 4 CUPS

BETA-CAROTENE HIGH

THE ELECTRIC ORANGE COLOR OF THIS DRINK, ESPECIALLY WHEN MADE
with fresh, in-season tangerine juice, is reason enough to drink it! Try it at 4 p.m.
instead of coffee. Carrot and orange make great partners—carrot cuts the acidity of
orange and adds body, while orange juice cuts the sometimes cloying sweetness of carrot
juice. Freshly squeezed fruit and vegetable juices are now more readily available from
a number of producers, both commercial and organic, at markets, delis, and specialty
stores. If you blend the juices with a banana, a two-inch cube of soft tofu, and a few
ice cubes, you will have a real nutrition booster.

1 part fresh orange juice	Pour equal amounts of both juices
1 part fresh carrot juice	into a tall glass and drink it down.
	It's too good to sip.

MAKES 1 DRINK

FROZEN HONEY LEMONADE AND LIMEADE

A TWIST ON THE STANDARD, AND GREAT ON A SWELTERING AFTERNOON.
For something so simple, your success depends on fresh juice and good-quality water. Because lemons and limes vary in sweetness, it is always a good idea to taste the drink and be ready to add more juice or honey depending on your palate. Also, if you are lucky enough to have a source for the sweet Meyer lemons, you will need practically no sweetening at all. Having been raised on Tupelo honey from Florida that my grandmother was convinced was particularly healthy, honey is a passion of mine. For lemonade, use a mild-flavored honey or, if you happen to have it, an orange honey would be great. I would shy away from darker, stronger-tasting honeys such as eucalyptus. Honey does not flow easily unless gently heated. It can also be difficult to mix into liquids and stay in suspension: no problem with a blender. If you have doubts about the flavor of your tap water, use bottled water.

1 oz honey
1 1/2 oz freshly squeezed
* lemon juice or*
* lime juice*
4 oz water
Generous 1/2 cup ice
Lemon or lime slice
* (optional), for garnish*

Put honey in a small measuring cup or other microwave-proof container and place in microwave oven. Microwave on high a few seconds until honey warms and will pour easily. Honey may also be warmed by placing jar in a saucepan of hot water.

Measure juice and water into blender container and add honey. Blend until well mixed. Add ice and blend again until mixture is slushy. Pour into a tall glass and garnish with lemon or lime slice, if desired.

MAKES 1 DRINK

HOMEMADE ORANGEADE

THIS RECIPE IS A GOOD EXAMPLE OF WHY TO MAKE FLAVORED SUGAR
syrups and have them available in the refrigerator. Where I live, fresh lemonade is
rarely available, even in good restaurants. Orangeade, never. I had forgotten such a
drink existed until I was making lemonade and wondered what it would taste like
made with orange sugar syrup instead of plain. Experiments went on from there. Just
orange sugar syrup and mineral water, plain or sparkling, is a wonderful, light drink on
its own. And with the addition of a little fresh juice, well, wow! These old-fashioned
drinks deserve more attention. Fresh orangeade is a delightful alternative to orange
juice and very refreshing for hot-sun-in-the-afternoon sipping.

¹/₂ oz Orange Sugar
Syrup (page 77)
1 tsp freshly squeezed
lemon juice
2 oz freshly squeezed
orange juice
4 oz water or
sparkling water

Measure orange syrup, lemon juice,
and orange juice into a tall glass.
Stir well and add ice to fill glass.
Stir again.

HOMEMADE LEMONADE: Follow the orangeade recipe, but increase the lemon juice to 1 ounce and omit
orange juice. If you only have plain sugar syrup, use 1¹/₂ tablespoons plain sugar syrup, 3 tablespoons
lemon juice, and 4 ounces water.

MAKES 1 DRINK

FRESH GINGER ALE

NOT ONLY IS GINGER SUPPOSED TO BE GOOD FOR YOU IN ALL SORTS
of ways, it has a decidedly cooling effect in summer. This is not like bottled ginger ale.
Instead it tastes spicy and sweet, like fresh ginger.

3 oz fresh ginger,
unpeeled
1 1/2 oz Plain or Orange
Sugar Syrup (page 76 or 77)
2 cups sparkling water
3 lime wedges

Cut ginger into rough pieces and chop very fine in a food processor. Scrape chopped ginger onto a double or triple thickness of cheesecloth and wring out juice into a small bowl. You should have about 2 ounces juice.

Add sugar syrup to ginger juice and stir well. Pour equal amounts over ice into 3 tall glasses. Add about 2/3 cup sparkling water to each. Stir, then squeeze a lime wedge over each drink and drop into glass.

MAKES 3 DRINKS

MADRAS

ICY PITCHERS OF ORANGE AND CRANBERRY JUICES MAKE ME HAPPY.
The combination is a great way to start the day, or break it at 11 a.m. Add vodka or
tequila if you want to stray from The Zone.

4 oz cranberry juice
1 oz freshly squeezed
orange juice
Lime wedge (optional)

Pour juices over ice in a short tumbler. Squeeze lime, if using, over drink and drop into glass. Stir.

MADRAS WITH SPIRITS: To juices, add 1 1/2 ounces vodka or tequila and a squeeze of lime.

MAKES 1 DRINK

SUGAR SYRUP

PLAIN AND FLAVORED SUGAR SYRUPS STORED IN THE REFRIGERATOR CAN be the answer to delicious, varied, and easy-to-prepare summer drinks (with or without alcohol), not to mention desserts, pancake syrups, and even sauces for such things as pork, duck, and chicken. They take very little time, keep well in the refrigerator, are often beautifully colored, aromatic, and inexpensive. What more could you ask?

PLAIN SUGAR SYRUP

EVERYTHING BEGINS HERE. THIS IS THE BASE FOR ALL THE FLAVORED syrups that follow. You may make the syrup in any amount as long as you keep the proportion of two parts sugar to one part water. I suggest you make the large amount of sugar syrup in this recipe, then portion it out by cupfuls to make several different flavors at once plus have some leftover plain sugar syrup.

4 cups sugar
2 cups water

Put sugar and the water in a heavy pot and bring to a boil over medium-high heat, stirring to dissolve sugar. Lower heat to regulate a moderate boil. With a brush dipped in water, wash down any sugar crystals clinging to the side of the pan. Boil 5 minutes, uncovered, without disturbing the mixture further. Remove from heat, let cool, then refrigerate in a covered container. Keeps indefinitely. If you plan on making orange or herb-scented sugar syrups, do not let the syrup cool.

ALMOND OR VANILLA SUGAR SYRUP: Follow recipe above and add about $1/2$ tablespoon almond or vanilla extract (use more or less to taste) to 1 cup cooled syrup.

MAKES ABOUT 3 CUPS

ORANGE SUGAR SYRUP

THIS QUICK METHOD PRODUCES A FRESH, TANGY ORANGE FLAVOR WITH a hint of bitterness. If you are sensitive to bitterness, you might want to blanch citrus zest in boiling water twice before using it. I like the little bite of bitterness. To me, it makes the fruit taste more like itself. But I do try to cut very fine zest with as little of the white pith attached as possible. You may use this method for any citrus zest— lemon, lime, grapefruit, even tangerine. Wash fruit well to make sure no wax is left on the peel, or buy unwaxed fruit.

1 cup hot Plain Sugar Syrup (previous page)
Zest from 3 medium oranges (or 3 lemons or limes), cut into very thin strips

Put hot sugar syrup and citrus zest into a blender container. Blend until pureed. Strain into a clean container and seal with a lid. Store in refrigerator. Will keep almost indefinitely.

CANDIED CITRUS ZEST: You might want to take a few extra minutes and make candied citrus zest. A by-product of your candy making is a citrus-flavored sugar syrup that you can use as you would any flavored syrup. Because the zest is cooked, this syrup has a different flavor than the fresh orange sugar syrup above. To make candied citrus zest, use the ingredient amounts above, but follow this method. Blanch the zest twice in a small amount of boiling water. Put blanched zest and 1 cup hot Plain Sugar Syrup in a small pot and heat over medium heat to a slow simmer. Cook until zest looks transparent, about 10 minutes. Strain zest from syrup, reserving syrup. Scatter zest on a rack to cool for 1 to 2 minutes. Then toss zest with 1/2 cup sugar on a plate, separating pieces with fingers and tossing until zest is well coated. Let zest cool several hours on a rack, then store in a tightly sealed container in a cool dark place. Keeps indefi-nitely, but best when used within the first few months. Strain cooking syrup into a covered container and refrigerate. Can also be stored indefinitely, but will eventually begin to crystallize. The timing on this is a mystery. Sometimes it happens very soon, sometimes not for weeks.

MAKES ABOUT 1 CUP

HERB-SCENTED SUGAR SYRUP

HERB-FLAVORED SUGAR SYRUPS CAN ADD REAL EXCITEMENT AND UNEX-
pected flavors to cocktails. Having them in the refrigerator may very well inspire you
to create many new concoctions. And they are such a beautiful green. I particularly
love having mint and pineapple sage available, but basil is another good one to try.
They make the most delicious herb-flavored lemonade and iced tea you can imagine.
And if you are lucky enough to have a lemon verbena bush, I envy you!

**1 1/2 cups tightly packed
fresh mint leaves,
pineapple sage, lemon
verbena, or basil**

**1 cup hot Plain Sugar
Syrup** (page 76)

Soft, green herbs such as mint and basil tend to oxidize and turn an ugly brown when bruised and cut, even if preserved in sugar syrup. To retard this, blanch the herbs first: Prepare an ice-water bath. Bring a pot of water to a boil and stir in herbs just to wilt them. Immediately drain and plunge herbs into ice bath to cool. Drain and squeeze out as much water as you can. Coarsely chop herbs.

Put hot sugar syrup and chopped herbs into a blender container. Blend until pureed. Strain into a clean container and seal with a lid. Store in refrigerator. Will keep about a week without oxidizing.

NOTE: These syrups have a higher solids content than plain and fresh orange syrup and therefore tend to crystallize sooner. They are not unhealthy to use once they have crystallized but they will no longer easily mix into a drink. However, you will probably use it up before you need to worry.

MAKES ABOUT 1 CUP

ALPHABETICAL INDEX BY DRINK NAME